KIDS IN HISTORY

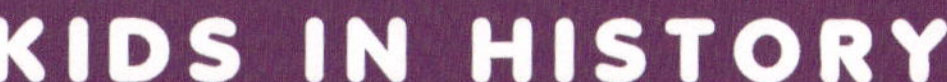

How Did Kids Live in Ancient Egypt?

BY MEGAN QUICK

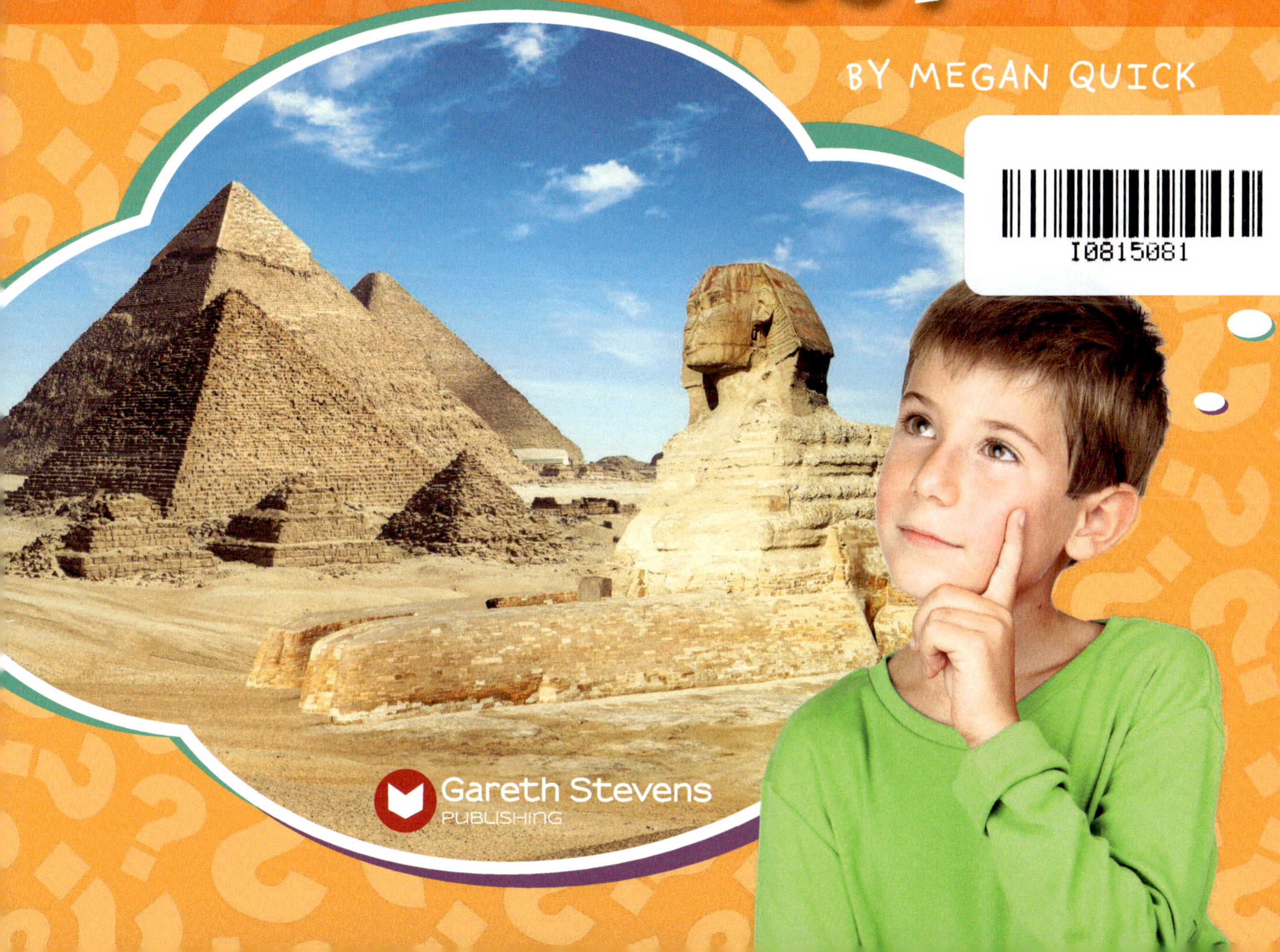

Gareth Stevens
PUBLISHING

Please visit our website, www.garethstevens.com. For a free color catalog of all our high-quality books, call toll free 1-800-542-2595 or fax 1-877-542-2596.

Library of Congress Cataloging-in-Publication Data

Names: Quick, Megan, author.
Title: How did kids live in ancient Egypt? / Megan Quick.
Other titles: Kids in history (Buffalo, N.Y.)
Description: Buffalo, New York : Gareth Stevens Publishing, 2024. | Series: Kids in history | Includes bibliographical references and index. | Audience: Grades 2-3
Identifiers: LCCN 2023008698 | ISBN 9781538288160 (library binding) | ISBN 9781538288153 (paperback) | ISBN 9781538288177 (e-book)
Subjects: LCSH: Children–Egypt–History–Juvenile literature. | Egypt–Social life and customs–To 332 B.C.–Juvenile literature.
Classification: LCC HQ792.E35 Q53 2024 | DDC 305.230932–dc23/eng/20230309
LC record available at https://lccn.loc.gov/2023008698

Portions of this work were originally authored by Sarah Machajewski and published as *A Kid's Life in Ancient Egypt*. All new material in this edition was authored by Megan Quick.

Published in 2024 by
Gareth Stevens Publishing
2544 Clinton Street
Buffalo, NY 14224

Designer: Jen Schoembs
Editor: Megan Quick

Photo credits: Cover (Pyramids), p. 1 (Pyramids) Merydolla/Shutterstock.com; cover (boy), p. 1 (boy) Gelpi/Shutterstock.com; cover (background), p.1 (background), series art (background) Login/Shutterstock.com; p. 5 Daily Travel Photos/Shutterstock.com; p. 7 Art Berry/Shutterstock.com; p. 9 (village) ZU_09 /iStock.com; p. 9 (wealthy house) duncan1890/iStock.com; p. 11 Macrovector/Shutterstock.com; p. 13 Cannasue/iStock.com; p. 15 (shirt) Rogers Fund 1925/commons.wikimedia.org, p. 15 (hair) Eloquence/commons.wikimedia.org, p. 15 (necklace) Rogers Fund and Edward S. Harkness Gift, 1922/commons.wikimedia.org; p. 17 Ihor Bondarenko/Shutterstock.com; p. 19 (both) Jaroslav Moravcik/Shutterstock.com; p. 21 (wrestling) Kurohito/commons.wikimedia.org, p. 21 (ball) World History Archive/Alamy.com.

Printed in the United States of America

CPSIA compliance information: Batch #CS24GS: For further information contact Gareth Stevens at 1-800-542-2595.

Contents

Words in the glossary appear in **bold** type the first time they are used in the text.

Ancient Times

Have you ever seen pictures of the **pyramids** in Egypt? Or the half-man, half-lion **statue** called the Great Sphinx? They are famous features of Ancient Egypt, a kingdom that began about 5,000 years ago. Can you imagine what it was like to live back then?

Ancient Egypt was one of the world's first **civilizations**. Kings, or pharaohs, ruled the land. Egyptians **worshipped** many gods. Everyday life was very different from ours today. Let's find out more about growing up in Ancient Egypt.

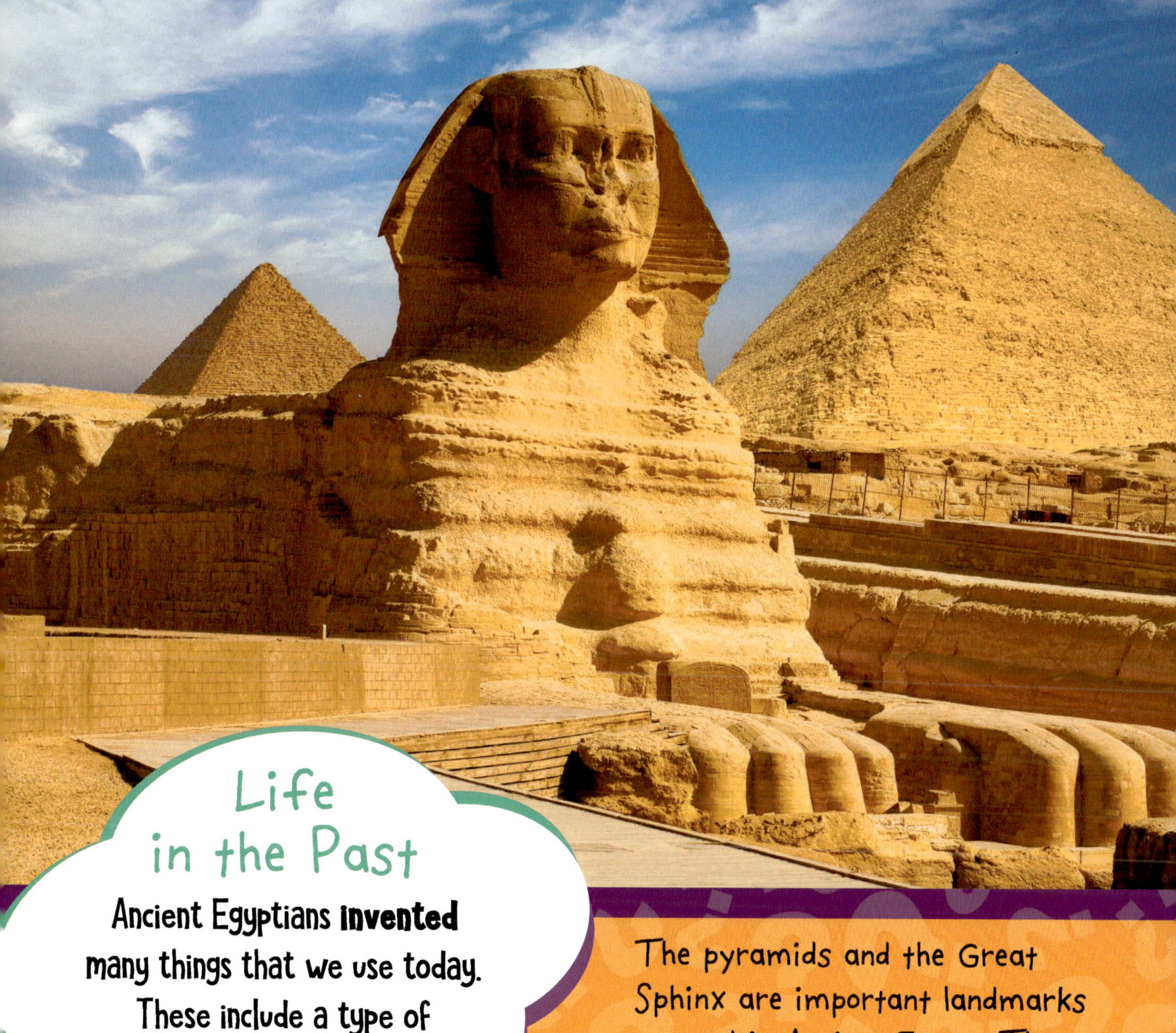

Life in the Past

Ancient Egyptians **invented** many things that we use today. These include a type of toothpaste, calendars, ink, and even bowling!

The pyramids and the Great Sphinx are important landmarks created in Ancient Egypt. The civilization lasted from about 3100 BCE to 30 BCE.

Life on the River

Life in Ancient Egypt depended on the Nile River. Most people lived near the river. The Nile provided water and rich soil for farming. It also acted as a kind of water freeway. Egyptians used the river to carry goods they traded with other civilizations.

Children growing up in Ancient Egypt spent a lot of time by the Nile. They might go fishing or help in the garden. But they also had fun in the river. Egyptian children learned how to swim at a young age.

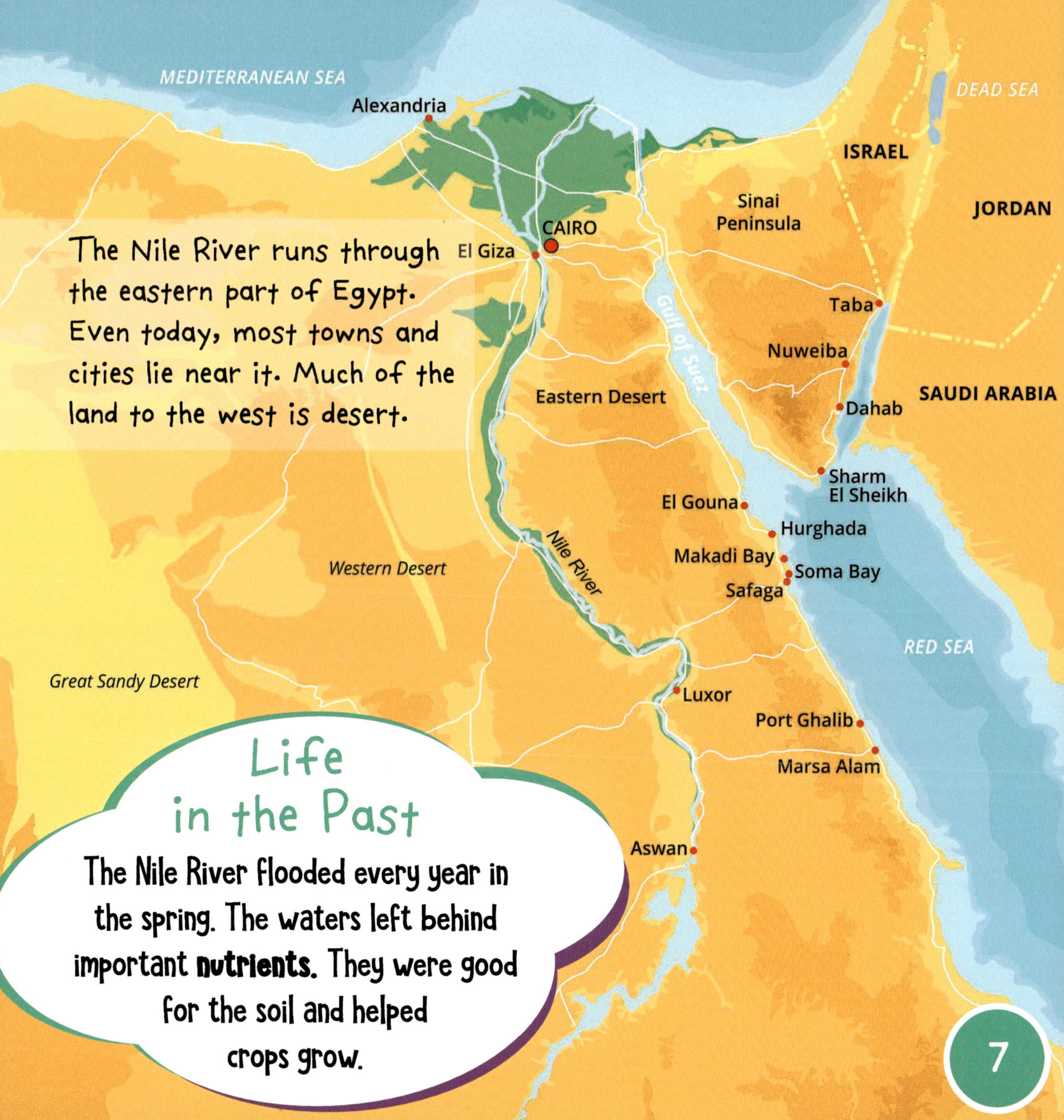

The Nile River runs through the eastern part of Egypt. Even today, most towns and cities lie near it. Much of the land to the west is desert.

Life in the Past

The Nile River flooded every year in the spring. The waters left behind important **nutrients**. They were good for the soil and helped crops grow.

Homes of the Rich and Poor

Everyone in Ancient Egypt was in a certain class. Kings and queens were at the top, while **peasants** and farmers were near the bottom. Their homes showed what class they belonged to. Kings and queens lived in fancy palaces. Their homes often included a temple as well.

Peasants' homes were very different. They used bricks made out of mud to build their houses. The roof was flat, and the floors were made of dirt. Small windows didn't let in too much heat from the sun. Entire families slept in one room.

Ancient Egyptian villages included simple houses with gardens. The homes of wealthy families were much grander.

Life in the Past

In wealthy homes, children lived with only their parents. In poor families, it was common for children to live in a house with uncles and cousins as well as their parents.

Egyptians at Work

Ancient Egyptians held many different jobs. Some were craftspeople. They made and sold cloth, tools, bricks, or **jewelry.** Many more were farmers. They worked on the land, preparing the soil, planting seeds, and gathering crops.

Children of farmers also worked hard. They helped out in the fields, planting and gathering. They traveled with their parents to other farms to trade food. Parents depended on their kids to help on the farm. Sons took over when their parents became too old or sick to work.

In the bottom half of this illustration, men and boys work in the fields at harvest time.

Time to Eat

Rich Egyptians enjoyed foods such as meat, fruit, and eggs. But farmers depended on the simple foods they grew themselves. They might grow crops such as grains, onions, beans, and figs. They also raised animals such as goats and sheep. They could fish in the Nile River for their dinner.

Egyptian women were in charge of cooking for the family. They had ovens of stone or clay where they prepared meals. Children ate bread often. Mothers made it with grain they grew on the farm.

Life in the Past

Ancient Egyptians did not have sugar. Instead, they used honey to sweeten food.

This drawing shows Egyptians hunting animals and then preparing the food.

What Kids Wore

It's hot in Egypt! In ancient times, people wore clothing that helped them stay cool. In fact, most children wore no clothes at all until age 6. Then, they wore simple clothing made from **linen.** Boys wore kilts, a type of skirt. Girls wore robes. People had sandals, but it was more common to go barefoot.

Egyptians' hairstyles also kept them cool. Boys shaved off their hair, sometimes keeping a lock on the side of the head. Girls wore their hair in braids. Children also wore jewelry.

Children wore shirts like the one on the top left. A child's necklace is shown on the bottom left. The hairstyle above was popular for boys.

Education in Egypt

Education in Ancient Egypt began at home. Mothers started teaching their children around age 4. At age 7, boys might begin attending school. The girls stayed home and learned skills such as cooking and cleaning. At age 14, many boys left school to learn their father's trade.

Not everyone knew how to read and write in Ancient Egypt. Those who did were called scribes. They read hieroglyphics, which is a kind of writing that uses pictures to stand for words or ideas. Scribes might become doctors or **priests.**

Life in the Past

Only children from rich families were able to attend school past the age of 14. Some poor families were not able to send their children to school at all. They needed to stay at home and work.

These Egyptian writings and drawings were done on **papyrus**. It became the paper we use today.

Gods and Mummies

Children in Ancient Egypt grew up learning about gods and goddesses. Egyptians believed these **divine** figures controlled all parts of their life, such as how much money they had and what the weather was like. They built temples to honor the gods and made offerings to keep them happy.

Ancient Egyptians also believed life continued after death. Pharaohs and queens were buried with objects they would need after they died. They were **preserved** as mummies so their dead bodies would stay lifelike.

King Tut's burial mask

Life in the Past

Only wealthy people could afford to be buried as mummies. Poor people buried their dead in the sand. The hot, dry sand did a good job of preserving the bodies.

King Tutankhamen, "King Tut," was a pharaoh from age 9 to 19. This picture shows how he was buried with his riches.

Enjoying Life

Life in Ancient Egypt could be hard work for children. But their parents also gave them time to have fun. Young Egyptians played sports, such as wrestling and gymnastics. They enjoyed music, dance, and reading. They even had their own board games.

Ancient Egyptians believed that life went on after death, so it was important to them that they lived life well. This began with their children, who learned, worked, and had fun. Childhood was an important stage for the people of this special civilization.

Life in the Past

Childhood in Ancient Egypt ended early. Girls were often married at the age of 12, while boys married at about 15.

Ancient Egyptian children enjoyed games and sports such as wrestling. They might play with a ball that looked like the one above.

Glossary

civilization: Organized society with written records and laws.

divine: Relating to a god.

invent: To create or produce something for the first time.

jewelry: Pieces of metal, often holding gems, worn on the body.

linen: A smooth, strong cloth or yarn made from flax.

nutrient: Something a living thing needs to grow and stay alive.

papyrus: Writing material made from the papyrus plant and used by ancient peoples.

peasant: A person at the bottom of society who worked the land.

preserve: To keep something in its original state.

priest: A person who performs religious ceremonies.

pyramid: A huge structure built in Ancient Egypt that has a square base and four triangular sides meeting at a point.

statue: A likeness that is sculptured, modeled, or cast in a solid substance.

worship: To honor or respect as a god.

For More Information

Books

Alexander, Heather. *A Child's Introduction to Egyptology: The Mummies, Pyramids, Pharaohs, Gods, and Goddesses of Ancient Egypt.* New York, NY: Black Dog & Leventhal Publishers, 2021.

O'Neal, Ciara. *Ancient Egypt Q&A: 175+ Fascinating Facts for Kids.* Emeryville, CA: Rockridge Press, 2021.

Websites

BBC Bitesize: Ancient Egypt
www.bbc.co.uk/bitesize/topics/zg87xnb
Check out activities, videos, and information about all parts of Ancient Egyptian life.

Ducksters: Ancient Egypt for Kids
www.ducksters.com/history/ancient_egypt.php
Learn more about the history, people, and culture of Ancient Egypt.

Fun Kids: Top 10 Facts About Ancient Egypt
www.funkidslive.com/learn/top-10-facts/top-10-facts-about-ancient-egypt/
Find out more fun facts about life in Ancient Egypt.

Publisher's note to educators and parents: Our editors have carefully reviewed these websites to ensure that they are suitable for students. Many websites change frequently, however, and we cannot guarantee that a site's future contents will continue to meet our high standards of quality and educational value. Be advised that students should be closely supervised whenever they access the internet.

Index